The Student Alphabet

D0166989

AN A-Z FOR STARTING UNIVERSITY

[fusion]

Cover design and Layout by
Intentional Design Co.
hello@iamintentional.co

Published by Fusion UK. Reprinted 2019

Fusion UK is a company limited by guarantee registered in England and Wales no. 3679369 and a registered charity No. 1073572.

Fusion Movement,
Unit 7, 30 Meadow Lane,
Loughborough,
LE11 1JY
01509 268 505
www.fusionmovement.org
hello@fusionmovement.org

Contents

Foreword

Fusion exists to see students find hope in Jesus and home in the local church.

We have guided tens of thousands of Christian students to start university well and be fully equipped for the adventure that lies ahead. The Student Alphabet is part of that preparation and contains the kind of advice that is often associated with the phrase, 'I wish I knew that before!'

I recommend you put the kettle on, make yourself a cup of tea and get comfortable. Our prayer is that in reading this little book you'll feel a lot less anxious about the transition to uni, and that the practical tips and advice will grow your confidence and fuel your excitement for what the university years hold.

Be inspired.

Rich Wilson
Fusion Movement Leader

Aargh to Alcohol

Aargh

We all have 'aargh' moments. You might be experiencing one now at the thought of university. So many questions - Where will I live? Who will I live with? Will I find good friends? Will I feel homesick? Will I be able to do the course? Will it be interesting? What about money and budgeting? How do I find a church? Questions that can race around our heads like runaway trains and leave us feeling anxious.

Relax, take a few deep breaths, say a short prayer and keep reading. Many have walked this way before. God is with you and is committed to guiding you down the right track.

Accountability

Accountability can be the difference between you becoming just another student, or making a difference for God in your university. Accountability is where you choose to share details of your life; your temptations and weaknesses, your struggles and dreams. You choose a person who you can trust and give them the permission to ask you how you are getting on and to challenge you. They may be the first point of contact when you need prayer for strength, or want to be open with when you mess up.

Every Christian student will do well to embrace this sort of accountability. These friendships will lead you into greater freedom and will encourage growth and consistency. I recommend that you find someone you would like to make yourself accountable to before university and as soon as possible once at university as well. If you feel you've already got naturally accountable relationships with people, then brilliant! Keep it up!

Arrival

Well done – you've made it! Arriving at university for the first time can be one of the most exciting or nerve-racking experiences you've had so far. It is normally both. But don't worry, help is close at hand. Fusion are a trusted guide and will point you in the right direction to find church connections and resources for the journey. It's worth remembering that on your first day, everyone is in the same boat. The nervous energy is high and people are keen to make the best first impression. Smile, be yourself, ask a few good questions, take time to listen and get involved.

Student Story

"Whatever you choose to do at university, do it on purpose. This applies to your attitude on everything; from dating to lectures, to money, to housework, to societies... The lifestyle you develop in your first few years of independence can stick with you for a long time, so make sure it's the lifestyle you want for yourself long-term, not just the one you think you're expected to have or the one you drifted into without thinking about it."

Michelle, Illustration, Loughborough University

Alcohol

This is a big one. Much of university social culture is based on alcohol. People use it to remedy their nerves and to loosen their inhibitions, especially when starting university. Why? Because they feel it makes them that little bit more confident, that little bit more adventurous, and perhaps that little bit funnier. However, if people are seeking alcohol to make them 'that little bit more' anything, then they are saying that who they are isn't good enough.

Our God is a God who loves to party! Too many times we forget this and go clubbing without him. Don't be afraid to be stone cold sober when surrounded by people who are drinking heavily. Place your confidence and identity in God, and enjoy the freedom of dancing the night away with a group of friends without the drama, confusion and hurt that alcohol can cause. It may feel awkward at first, but sober nights out get easier and more fun with practice.

Let me challenge you. If you haven't yet got to university, I challenge you to go through Freshers' Week without alcohol! Be known as a Christian who loves to party and is one of the first on the dance floor, but who doesn't need to be drunk in the process. You will confuse, challenge, and inspire people; there's no doubt about that. If you're already at university, try a few weeks without alcohol to remind yourself that you don't need it. If you find that difficult, then rise to the challenge and take a few months off alcohol to combat that little bit of addiction. At university you'll see first-hand the destructive effects that alcohol can have. You'll learn of friends having sexual encounters with people whilst drunk, trying substances they'd never touch sober, and waking up with injuries and no memory of the night before. Be the person who can drink responsibly. Who has fun and a good dance, but is the first to look after a drunk friend and carry a mate home.

If you are drinking, be aware of how much and what you're drinking. Leaving your drink unattended carries the risk of it being spiked. It's better to be safe, and a good choice is to only drink what you've seen being made rather than whatever's handed to you.

Student Story

"During my first year, not long after Christmas, I decided to go on an alcohol fast for 40 days and give the money I saved to a charity. It was a great way to sharpen up a bit. I feel like, often, giving something up can do that. It also helped me to remember that I can have a good time without any alcohol and do something good for other people as well."

Daniel, Law, Coventry University

Balls to Budgeting

Balls

Think Cinderella not juggling. Balls are a grown up version of a high school prom and are a fantastic opportunity to see your friends all dressed up in something other than the average going out outfits - elegant dresses for girls and black tie for boys. Ticket prices may cause your eyes to water, but it is often worth it. Let's face it; most of us love to dress up a little bit posh every now and again.

Banking

Banks will be waiting to lure you into their student accounts offering you attractive bonuses for joining their bank. I once took a second account just because they offered me a free popcorn machine! Before you allow yourself to be lured into using a certain bank because of the student railcard they offer, or the attractive cashback promise, look into the small print. This may seem boring and tedious but you will save yourself being caught out later on. Here are some practical hints and tips:

- Look for a student account. These often offer free overdrafts and a bonus for signing up.

- Don't be fickle, one bank might offer a more attractive bonus, but their scheme may not be as suitable for your needs.

- Read about the ethical policy of the bank. Whilst the words ethical and banking don't always fit together, some banks are at least trying.

- Look for an interest free overdraft, and think about the amount you may need. Will you be working to support yourself? Will your parents be supporting you?

- Look at the graduate schemes they run. If you have an overdraft, some banks start charging interest as soon as you've graduated, whereas others allow you a larger interest free overdraft for a couple of years, to give you time to get onto your feet, and pay it back without interest.

- Avoid credit cards; you don't need that kind of additional debt.

- When opening the account, don't immediately increase your overdraft to the maximum amount. Think about how you can be a good steward with money, and remember that the overdraft is not your money! Everything you spend from a loan or overdraft will need to be paid back. Think about making yourself accountable to someone in the area of finances.

See also Budgeting

Bills

Yes, bills, those dreaded things nobody really wants to take responsibility for and which often end up unopened in a pile by the door or in a drawer. I urge you to open bills as soon as they arrive. This may be your phone bill or a utility bill if you are living in a house. Sort them out and pay them as soon as possible so they don't become niggling thoughts in the back of your mind.

If you are living in a house, or looking to live in a house, have a think and a chat with your housemates about whether you want a house in which bills are included in your rent or not. Take into account how many people are living in your house. You could even be strategic and ask the previous occupants how much their average bill comes to. You will certainly come to realise why you are told to switch lights off at home and turn the heating off when it's not needed. If you're living in a house in which the bills are included, don't feel that this allows you to go 'all out' and leave the heating on all day. Be respectful to the fact that someone is footing the bill at the end of the month and you can be doing your bit for the environment, and be mindful of caps on how much you can spend.

Boundaries

Boundaries are not a boring or restricting thing! They are self imposed rules for living well that are based around our values. They help you make good decisions and to be confident in yourself, no matter what unexpected circumstances arise. How do your values affect your boundaries? Have you already decided how you're going to react before someone is offering you more to drink than you want to? Or before someone is flirting with you? Or before your boyfriend/girlfriend comes to stay for the weekend etc.? Where do you need to put some new boundaries in place for your time at university?

See also Accountability

Bubble

Most students are not part of the bubble and most Christians don't intend to get stuck in the bubble; it often happens without thinking. The bubble is a place where some Christian students can spend all their time. Being surrounded by Christians 24-7 is an attractive and comfortable place to be, where it's easy to make friends and be in community, but it can become an insular and stagnant environment. So how do you pop the bubble?

Take some time to think and pray about the friends God would love you to share your life with, join a club or society and make a point of socialising with people outside of church and inviting these new friends to church or a small group. Church community is essential and will help you live a balanced life of engagement with those who don't share your values and provide the whole life discipleship to keep growing in your faith.

See also Love and Mates

Budgeting

Budgeting is something we often plan to do, but never actually get round to it. University can be a great time where we can learn a lot about money. Some of us will feel the worry of reaching the end of a large overdraft, whereas others might be helped out by their parents. Either way, budgeting is a necessary skill to learn and a good discipline to adopt. Don't wait until you find your debit card is rejected before you decide that it would be a good idea to keep on top of things financially.

One piece of common sense is to always be aware of your bank balance. I have spent many months dodging the sweat-inducing 'show balance' button on cash machines only to find myself in a bit of trouble! Ignorance is not always bliss.

Draw up a spreadsheet, label it 'budgeting' and get to work. Think about what goes in and out each month and whether you have any direct debits to pay each month. Then think about what you have been spending so far. Think about your week. Here are some ideas to prompt you:

House payments:	Rent
	Bills
Other Payments:	Phone Bill
	Food Bill
	Snacks
Social:	Club Entry
	Travel
	Drinks whilst socialising
	Meals out
Personal:	Clothing
	Toiletries
	Music
	Subscriptions (e.g. Netflix)
	Giving

I recommend that you do this as soon as you can, rather than leaving it until the end of a year or term. Many students find it helpful to open a second bank account and transfer only the amount from their loan that they are going to need for that month. That way the larger bank balance at the start of the year doesn't tempt them into overspending early on. It helps to keep finances in perspective. Here are some practical tips for you to think about:

- Don't just extend your overdraft to the largest amount possible. Everything you spend will need paying back at some point.

- Try taking your weekly budget out in physical cash. It will help you keep in mind how much you have left and avoid overspending.

- Keep receipts so you know what and when you have spent. It will also help overcome any confusion when you get your bank statement.

- Always open your financial post. Never let a pile of unopened post accumulate. Shops and banks do make mistakes, and we need to keep an eye on our statements for safety, especially in the case of card fraud.

- Think before you buy. Ask yourself, 'Do I really need it?' This simple question can save expensive impulse spending.

- Take advantage of the discounts that your student card allows!

- When shopping for essentials ensure you are always getting the best deal. Buy one half price is only useful if you'll actually use both items!

Finally, be a good steward of your money. If you have a bit of a weakness for shopping, make yourself accountable to someone (see accountability). Also, just because you are a student living off of a loan, doesn't mean you can't give financially to your church. Work out the money you spend on yourself, and give a percentage of that.

Student Story

"I knew a student who spent £950 in the first two days of receiving his funding. The rest of the year was a money stress for him. You can feel pretty good when you have a good sum of money in your account; especially if it's for the first time. The tendency is to spend huge chunks and not think about your cash flow, but now is the time to learn to be smart with your money."

Jack, Theology, Cambridge

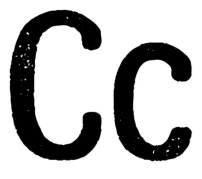

Cc

Calling to Coursework

Calling

Your calling starts now. It involves both who you are becoming and what you will do with your life. It is about doing what is in front of you to the best of your ability and also thinking about what lies ahead. Your calling will impact your career choices and be the compass for your direction in life. Although it might feel ages away, you can start to research career options, volunteering and work placement opportunities now. Your department or library is normally a good place to start. Most people don't have a really clear idea about what they are going to do, so university provides an opportunity to explore some things. You can test yourself in different environments, see what you enjoy and are good at, and what things leave you feeling fully alive. Don't wait until you graduate, you are called today.

See also Work Experience

Student Story

"Make the most of the big events on campus like Freshers' Fair and Careers Fairs. You can find out loads of information about where you're now living, what you might want to do in the future and above all else you can pick up some amazing free stuff. I get all my pens from these events!"

Mark, Management Sciences, Loughborough University

Christian Union

Most universities will have some sort of Christian Union - a place for students from a host of different churches across the town or city to meet, pray and worship together. These tend to vary greatly in size and activity, but are very focused on mission on campus and a great place to support and encourage each other and find out about what's going on in the wider church across your uni town. They're likely to run events throughout the year which are great to invite your mates to.

Christianity

Say the word 'holiday' and people think of sunshine and beaches, say 'Father Christmas' and they think of a red suit and mince pies. Say the word 'Christianity' to a friend and ask them what their initial thoughts are. I recently asked my friend and her words were, 'church, nice people, restrictions, rules, boring talks, Sunday school, hymns and boring songs'. In past surveys 'judgemental' and 'unfriendly' are also other words students have used.

The reality is that many students have no real idea what Christianity is about, they have never been to church and haven't spent time with someone who loves Jesus. This is why your time at university can be a game changer for you, for fellow students, and for showing what it really means to be a Christian. The generation of students arriving today are open minded and curious and there is lots of opportunity to show and tell people what Christianity is all about. It is time to dismantle the old stereotypes, frozen perceptions and outdated opinions, and work to 're-brand' Christianity on campus.

Our lives can be lived in such a way that when people hear the word 'Christian' their immediate thoughts are 'loving, kind, forgiving, generous, fun, authentic and passionate'. How can we do this? By being genuinely loving, outrageously kind, openly forgiving, extravagantly generous, full of fun, consistently authentic and infectiously passionate. And through this, showing people that Jesus is worth loving and living for.

**Student
Story**

"I remember that I didn't make it clear that I was a Christian to a lot of people in my halls. Then when I went to a Freshers' welcome service as a second year I saw a guy who used to live in my halls at the service too. We were both Christians but neither of us knew that the other one was a Christian. I'm not saying you need to be 'shouting off the rooftops' and telling everyone you meet. I'm just saying be you, live as a disciple of Jesus would and be proud to know Jesus."

**Tasha, Youth and Community Work, University of
Bedfordshire**

Christmas

As a first year student, Christmas is your first proper time back at home since flying the nest. For some, you'll be excited about spending a bit of time with your family, for others family life is not so straightforward. Being used to independence means coming back home can feel claustrophobic and questions like 'have you made your bed today?' or 'where are you off to tonight?' are a little annoying.

You may have left home as a child, but choose to come back as a young adult. Make sure that you don't first enter the house with a huge bag of washing, or with immediate plans to leave and catch up with your buddies. Instead, realise that you will have been really missed, and that your family would love to hear all about your last three months. Divide your time carefully between people you want to see, and people who want to see you, not just the people who will cook you up the best Christmas dinner (although we realise that is very important)!

Church

Church works best when we recognise that we don't go to church, we are the church. The Apostle Paul describes us as a body where we all have a part to play. Finding a local church community at university that is right for you is a number one priority.

We can choose churches like we choose universities, picking a place where we can thrive and grow, a place where we can learn, a place where we can get stuck-in and become a part of the community. The church is a family, which means that it's also somewhere we serve and help to shape. Throughout our lives the church will be there to support, teach, challenge and be a community to invite others into.

Download the Student Linkup app

Student Linkup will connect you to churches near to your university. It will help you to see what churches are nearby, what they're like and who to connect with there. Use the app and the Fusion website to research the churches near your university. Churches will also use it to contact you before you even leave home!

Student Linkup is available in the App or Play store, or online at www.studentlinkup.org

Before you arrive at university, decide you are going to visit a church the first Sunday you are there. Don't dither around for weeks, allowing yourself to get distracted. The very first Sunday, go to a local church! Pray about it and if you feel that it is the right place for you, make the decision to commit and get stuck-in. If it's not right, keep meeting with other local churches until you find a church to call home. But don't delay committing to find a place where you can put down roots, you should try hard to establish yourself in a new church home before the Christmas break.

Student Story	*"Get searching for a church before you arrive at uni. Don't leave it a few weeks, because that'll soon turn into months and you'll never get settled. The best way to feel a part of a new church is to get stuck in early!"*
	Mark, Management Sciences, Loughborough University

Clothes

Are you in the shops all the time, chasing the next vogue fashion, or can you make one top last three years? Do you make your own clothes or do you share and swap? Do you think carefully about your outfit each day or do you chuck on the first thing you see? Do you wash and fold, turn inside out, upside down (any way that you can't see that chilli sauce stain from the kebab on Friday)?

Clothes – we all wear them! But how much of our identity is intrinsically linked with what we wear. How much of our money goes on clothes? Do we hoard, or do we give away what we don't wear? Do we chase the next top or pair of shoes believing that it will complete our wardrobe? Does everything have to have a label on it? What is the ethical or environmental impact of the clothes we wear?

We like to call ourselves poor students, but actually that is one big fib! We live in one of the wealthiest parts of the globe and rarely contemplate how many of yesterday's luxuries have become today's necessities. Before you buy, think! Do you need it? Will you wear it? Do you have two others like it? Do you really need it in another colour? I encourage you to think about your attitudes to clothes and the part they play in your life. We live in a culture where we are told that 'things' complete us. Are you buying into this?

Clubs

Big clubs, little clubs, seedy stick-to-the-floor clubs. You might be a 'dancer', you might be a 'stand-and-chatter', or you may be an 'I'd-rather-be-watching-TVer'. Either way, like them or loathe them, nightclubs tend to play a large part in the socialising of students. We're called to be in the world but not of the world. So, enjoy the fun and friendship that clubbing has to offer without joining in with unhealthy thoughts, beliefs and behaviours about alcohol, identity and relationships. Show people that you don't need a few beers before you can throw some shapes on the dance floor. In a culture where many people don't consider a good night out a 'good night out' unless they have gotten drunk or got with someone, show people that you can have a brilliant time without the hangovers and the embarrassing kiss-and-tell stories.

Maybe, gather together a group of people who love God and love clubbing and start a club ministry team! Go out and pray for people dancing, pray for the DJ and staff, keep your eyes open for opportunities to serve and love; caring for someone who is being sick, getting them water, helping them out, getting friends home safely.

We follow a party deity and John 2:1-11 gives us an insight into a God who loves to party and who loves helping people out in difficult or embarrassing situations.

Colds

I need to educate you on 'freshers' flu'! So many people are coming from all different areas of the country, even the world, each bringing with them a new set of colds or viruses that you have not yet encountered or built up immunity to. This, teamed with late nights, lack of sleep and a new environment, make for a perfect breeding ground for horrible colds and viruses.

It isn't always easy to eat properly and to get sufficient sleep. However, a little bit of self discipline and being kind to yourself means that if you do encounter one of these little terrors then your body will be in better shape for fighting it off nice and fast! Make an effort to eat your five-a-day and pack some max strength lemsip just in case.

Contact

Technology makes it easy for us to stay in contact and that is a really good thing. We want to share enough of our lives to allow friends and relatives to feel connected, but not so much as we have nothing new to share when we get to catch up face to face. Too much contact can also make us over dependant, part of growing up means that we don't share every problem we encounter with our parents. We also want our contact to be about sharing and giving, do we just make contact when we need something?

Many students have found that a WhatsApp group has been an ideal way to share the right information with the right people. Alternatively, and counter-culturally, you could even try hand-written letters because the extra time and personal touch can be so worth it, especially when you receive one back!

See also WhatsApp

Coursework

Leave it until the last minute so the pressure kicks in, or complete it in the long view of a deadline? Either way, it needs to be done. Leave as much time as you can to ensure that you can allow for any changes to be made. Ensure that when you hand in a piece of coursework you can be proud that you have done it to your best ability.

Remember how your teachers used to nag you to read through your work a couple of times before you gave it in? I used to roll my eyes at that suggestion, yet doing a degree has taught me that you are not just sacrificing the quality of your work when you don't take the time to read it over, you are also sacrificing marks! Ouch! If grammar and spelling is not your strong point, ask a friend to read over it for you. With fresh eyes, they may be able to spot the things you couldn't.

Dd

Dating to Drugs

Dating

Our culture often puts people into couples. There is always speculation on who is getting with who, putting huge pressure on celebrities, but even more pressure on us! The media message is we're not complete without a partner. This can also be the subtle message in our churches. Whether someone is right or wrong for us seems to matter less than having somebody on our arm. The truth is that it is God who completes us, who desires to be the centre of our world.

If you are dating someone, then ensure that God is central to the relationship. Pray together and talk about your relationship with God together. Be aware that your relationship is also a witness to your friends, hall and coursemates. Show them what a relationship looks like with God at the centre. Show them how you can balance your time between your relationship and your friends.

If you aren't dating someone then you have more time to push into your relationship with God. Pursue him like you would pursue another person. Allow God to mould you into the person someone else would want to date, rather than looking for the person who fits you now.

Daytime TV

Daytime TV is a surprisingly attractive black hole. You start watching ironically and before you know it you're so into Murder, She Wrote it's unreal. This is a whole new realm of TV to explore but be aware how quickly it can sap your time – there are so many great opportunities to be grasped at uni, don't lose out on real relationships and adventures to the draw of bad perms and shocking storylines.

Deadlines

There are probably four types of people when it comes to deadlines.

Type one – Hand in a Week Early:
You know all the deadlines before you have even started the module; you attend every lecture, pre-printed lecture notes in hand and a variety of different highlighters available. You do the extra reading and are well acquainted with the library. Whilst everyone else is feeling the stress you are kicking back with a nice cup of tea, as cool as a cucumber before reaching for the textbook for the next piece.

Most likely to: get a first

Type two – Deadline Dodger:
You sweat at the thought of impending deadlines, your stress levels sky rocket and every little thing becomes a procrastination technique. Suddenly cleaning your room seems a very attractive prospect, and it seems vital that your sock drawer is colour coded. You are first to apply for an extension when, let's face it, you could have done the work and left your room alone.

Most likely to: become popular with the housemates by always having the kettle on because every moment is a tea break moment.

Type three – Deadline, What Deadline?:
You are living life in a state of ignorance which seems like bliss until you wonder

why people are frantically rushing around you. Your world is brought swiftly back down to earth when you hear the sentence, 'Oh! Didn't you know our coursework is due in tomorrow!?' You then spend the next 24 hours draped over a textbook you didn't even know existed.

Most likely to: do a disappearing act, and emerge a day later with huge under-eye bags and a piece of coursework.

Type four – Pressure Goes On, Work Gets Done:

You are fully aware of deadlines, you know they exist and when they are. You even know exactly what you have to do for them. However, you do little about it until the last moment when you are seen down the local shop buying a six-pack of Red Bull and a bumper box of Pro-Plus. You get the work done, yes, but to the best of your ability? Well that is debatable.

Most likely to: have a caffeine twitch!

Student Story

"Looking back on uni life, my best piece of advice is to make a timetable for your life – I think the grown up word is a 'diary'. It may sound boring, but you'll fit loads more in, get work done on time and have a lot less stress. A diary stops you feeling like you have to spend ages doing work and pull 'all-nighters' to know you're working hard. Timetabling in leisure, work, exercise and other stuff means that you're more consistent, rather than binging when deadlines come knocking and having to drop everything you like doing."

Jamie, Geoscience, University of Bristol

Debt

For many students it is inevitable that you will leave university with a significant amount of debt to your name. With tuition fees increasing it may feel overwhelming, but don't panic. You don't have to start paying back the loan until you graduate and are earning more than a certain amount of money and it isn't going to be with you forever. The debt is cancelled if you haven't paid it back after too long. However, the loans are not free, they accumulate interest and if it takes 25 years to pay off, you could end up paying back over £80,000 in total. If you're going to spend that much money, you may as well make the most of your time at uni! Whatever your financial situation, there are a number of things you can do to make good decisions with the money you have. Ask yourself these questions:

- Who do you owe money to at the moment? Can you make a plan to pay them back without it dragging on for too long?

- Are there any excesses in your life?

- Do you need an interest free overdraft on your student account? They are offered but they have to be paid back one day. You do have the option to take the account but ask for the overdraft facility to be removed, or at least reduced.

- Think twice about signing up to long mobile phone contracts. Could you get a sim-only deal?

- Can you get a part time job whilst at university to avoid getting into too much debt?

- Be accountable: can you find a 'money mentor'? For a couple of weeks, write down everything you purchase or spend your money on and take it to them.

- Consider using a budgeting tool, look at www.themoneycharity.org.uk

Above all, don't be anxious about your finances. If you feel like you're in trouble, speak to someone about it quickly. There is plenty of assistance available to help people get their finances back on track.

See also Budgeting

Deposits

You might have to pay a room bond or house deposit when you first move into new accommodation. Make sure your landlord puts your deposit in a government-backed tenancy deposit scheme (TDS). In order to get that back when you leave, remember to take good photos, notes and details of any wear or damage before you move in (think about those marks and scuffs on the walls and floors!). Get them checked over by the landlord, if possible, so that they don't try and charge you later. Take good care of your rooms and watch out with putting posters up if they're going to leave Blu Tack marks!

Discipleship

We are not content to simply be converts to the Christian faith, we want to be passionate disciples of Jesus Christ; men and women who are actively learning to become more like Jesus. Disciples are made, not born, and they are made through the process of discipleship.

Discipleship should be at the very centre of church life. It's what Jesus was most concerned about and it is the main way to grow as a Christian. There is great teaching available to help us on this journey, but our own experience tells us that an accumulation of knowledge does not automatically transform us. Having someone help us to apply that knowledge, believe in us and invest in us does transform us.

Discipleship can take place in a variety of different ways and is a combination of attitude and activity. The attitudes that facilitate discipleship are: a willingness to learn, a willingness to change and a willingness to receive from others. The activities that facilitate discipleship are many and varied, but I believe that one of the most effective ways to be discipled is to be in a discipling friendship with someone who is a little further on in their own journey with Christ.

Make it your aim during university to be on a deliberate discipleship journey that deepens your friendship with God.

Discounts

Student discounts are often 10-20% and can make a big difference to your final costs. Ask shops, restaurants and services at the till and they might offer you a discount, even if it's not advertised! Also note that some shops will need to see your student card.

See also Shopping

Dissertation

The funny thing is, you probably haven't even given a thought to your dissertation but you have learnt to fear that word! You have recognised the mutterings and groaning of your third-year friends over this so called 'dissertation'. All you know is that it is the mother of all coursework and it is apparently scary (and you don't even know what it involves yet). Well, let me quieten your heart on this one because I'd hate to think of you fearing it like I did.

A dissertation is a piece of coursework often ranging between 6,000 to 15,000 words done over a period of time (often the majority of a term, including a holiday). It is often focused on one topic of a subject, generally one you can decide yourself. It has to be presented in an academic format and bound together. I advise you to stick to any proposed deadlines that your tutor presents as they have had years of practice. Don't be afraid to ask for help and gather all relevant research once you have decided on your title. Also, adopt a work hard, play hard mentality. Set specific times and days on which to focus on the dissertation, and times in which to relax and socialise promising yourself to try and not think about it! Set realistic targets over long and short periods of time, e.g. 500 words to be done by the end of the day.

Finally, remember that you will have studied for 2-3 years before doing your dissertation so don't let it scare you now. You will have racked up plenty of knowledge and resources by that time. Your ability will be sufficient, and if you are struggling at all, there are plenty of strategies in place to give extra help for no cost (consult your student advice centre for more information). All in all, work hard and enjoy your dissertation; it will be a piece of work that you can cherish for years to come! Mine is nicely bound and kept in a safe place, it is kind of satisfying to know that I researched and completed it to the best of my ability.

Doorstop

A doorstop keeps your door open! An open door says to people you are sociable and friendly. Buy or make a doorstop to take to uni, you never know who might need a friendly chat!

Drinking Games

Universities are cracking down on drinking games, however, you may still find yourself in an environment where these are taking place.These are common freshers' week bonding techniques and can be hard to stay out of. On top of the excessive drinking, the games themselves, 'have you ever...', for example, can leave you sharing things you'd actually rather others not know. One option is to join in with an alternative non-alcoholic drink; others might choose to hang out with those playing but not take part in the game. The core thing to ask yourself is, 'how can I build relationships with people without having to compromise myself?' Think, discuss and decide how you are going to deal with things like this before you even arrive at uni.

See also Alcohol and Accountability

Drugs

University can be a time for experimenting in many different things as there is such a variety of backgrounds entering into one culture and a new freedom away from home. For some it will definitely be sex, drugs and rock and roll! This is potentially more of a challenge for Christians who are into music and the clubbing scene. Keep your eyes open and educate yourself on the effects of drug use and reasons for addiction. Many people try drugs at university but do not get addicted, whereas some people will begin addictions which they take on into later life.

As a Christian do not back away from friends who are experimenting with drugs, just continue to love them and be a friend. Learn to articulate why God is sufficient for you without coming across as judgemental. Be open about it and pray with people if drugs are affecting your friendship circle.

Easter Holiday to Execs

Easter Holiday

The chances are you will probably get to your Easter Break and wonder how you got there so fast! With only one term left until the whole year is finished you will be in your second year before you know it. Take the time to look over the last semester and reflect over what you have been up to, and the changes that have happened within your character and your life. Make some goals for the semester ahead. Is there someone you have been putting off sharing your faith with? Have you committed fully to your church? Enjoy your break, celebrate Easter, and return to uni feeling refreshed and ready to go again.

Ear Plugs

In some halls and houses, especially in your first year, it might be loud and noisy with people coming back at various times throughout the night. A quiet night's sleep is what we all crave. If the neighbours are noisy, buy some ear plugs or politely ask them to quieten down if it happens too often.

Evangelism

80% of people become Christians because they know someone who is. Friendship evangelism is especially effective in the student culture because it is so easy to get to know people and there are plenty of opportunities to chat. The few years of being a student are often the most fruitful years of your life for friendship evangelism.

How do we become more effective in friendship evangelism? Here are some ideas:

- Learn to identify with people who are not Christians, be interested in them and find common ground.

- Listen to people, make them feel valued, care for them and serve them.

- Ask God for his compassion for people and his urgency to know them.

- Provoke friends by our lifestyle, and the things we say about who God is and what he does today in our lives.

- Pray for our friends!

The motivation for evangelism must come from loving our friends and outworking this love in proclamation, action and signs.

See also Words, Works and Wonders

Student Story

"I'd really encourage you to be real in sharing your faith; evangelism doesn't have to be weird, like some religious add-on to your normal life. I was worried when my friend said he wanted to come and check out my church. It's all a bit lively, hands in the air, that kind of thing. Actually, afterwards, he said it was like 'a football match' and not long after that ended up making a commitment to Jesus. I think the best thing to do is be real and natural about your faith as part of your everyday life."

Jonny, Criminology, University of Westminster

Exams

The chances are that if you are reading this book, you already have a fairly good idea about what exams are about. Remember that God wants to be involved in every facet of your life and that includes your study. He will not sit your exams for you, but before you revise why not get into the habit of praying for concentration and committing the revision session to him!

Remember the important things like getting a good amount of sleep, eating well, writing a revision timetable with enough breaks and try and find some time to catch up with friends, even if it's just for a lunch break or an episode of your favourite TV show.

Execs

Your Students' Union will probably have a team of executives, often students that are voted in to represent the university's students and their opinions and values. If you get a chance to vote in this selection, try not to just be tempted by their amazing fancy dress costume, fancy posters and the amount of sweets they give out. Look at their manifesto and vote based on their ideas and the things you value. If you're really passionate about this you could get involved in the union activities and campaigns yourself!

Beyond the Students' Union exec all the clubs and societies have exec positions and opportunities to grow and develop in leadership.

Falling Out to Friendships

Falling Out

During your school years, in the midst of friendship group fallouts, gossip and blame shifting, you might think 'I can't wait until university. Everyone will be so much more mature and grown up. I can leave all this behind'. This might not be the case.

Looking back at my university years, it was only in my final year that I put together strategies of dealing with confrontation. I wish I had done it earlier. My strategy is simple but effective application of Matthew 5:18. If you have a problem with a person, think and pray about it, and then gently confront the person as soon as you can. Often you will find that there has been a misunderstanding.

Jesus didn't let people walk all over him, he didn't hold his tongue all of the time, especially when there was injustice. Sometimes we need to look inside ourselves and ask why we are reacting in a certain way. Is it an irrational response, or tied into our own inadequacies and insecurities rather than that of the other party? If not, act maturely and with careful thought. Although this might take some practice, you will find that people are more comfortable around you because you are open and honest.

Family

You may miss your family and desire to go home at every opportunity. On the other hand you may love university so much that you barely give home a fleeting thought. Either way, it is important that you maintain a relationship with your parents and siblings. Make it a habit to speak to them at least once a week. Don't forget that even though your life has changed drastically, it is most likely that there will be a you-shaped hole back at home.

However, if your student railcard is getting used every weekend to flee from university, have a think about why you always desire to rush off at every opportunity. Are you not enjoying university? Do you not like the people you have been placed with? Are you not enjoying your course? If you can relate to any one of these questions, then realise that you are not alone. It is important to speak to people; your course tutor or hall warden, or even student welfare. It isn't the end of university, accommodation can be changed, as can courses. Often it is around feeling connected to other people, and if this is the case consider joining a club, going to church or volunteering with others. Jump at the chance of meal invites and church socials. Get a good network of people around you who you can invest into.

See also Homesickness

Fancy Dress

Fancy dress is likely to be a theme which runs throughout your university life. It's popular because it's fun and a great way to get people together and have a laugh.

You will find yourself scheduled in for a good number of fancy dress socials, be that dressing up as an Oompa Loompa or a Television set! When searching for outfits, pop to your local charity shop instead of spending tens of pounds on shop bought outfits. Buy cheap things that you can rip up and adapt, because you might not need that Snowman outfit again! When a bit of paint is going to make that outfit just that little bit more realistic, be aware of your surroundings if you want to see that hall/house deposit again! Plus, if painting on skin, ensure that it is easily washed off unless you fancy doing that presentation with last night's drawn on tiger stripes still stubbornly adorning your face.

"Buy a bed sheet. It will cover every fancy dress party ever."

Michelle, Illustration, Loughborough University

Fire Alarms

They will happen. Most likely in your first week and most likely in the early hours of the morning. Some will be drills and some might even be real alarms. Don't be grumpy if it happens at 3am and again at 5am, it is all part of starting uni, just make sure you have a dressing gown or hoody ready to put on as you have to stand out in the cold for a little while!

Food

Eating well on a student budget is achievable! Become good friends with the reduced section in supermarkets. Find out when market day is and grab some fresh seasonal food and knocked down prices at the end of the day. Invest in community and share your shopping, food and cooking needs with another friend or group of friends. This saves you money and time and you may find you eat better when you are cooking for more than one. When I eat alone, laziness means that I go for convenience food and the fact that I have no desire to impress myself with my culinary skills means that it is often bland and simple.

However, watch me come to life when I have another person to cook for. I will start straying away from the microwave and move towards the oven, or even the wok! Plus, I actually enjoy stopping and eating much more when I have someone to chatter to between mouthfuls. Throughout the Bible there are many situations in which people spend time together around food. It is the context for fellowship and faith and it is particularly true in the life of Jesus. It is God's design for sharing life together. So find a friend or two, leave the microwave alone and enjoy your meal times.

See also Online Food Shopping

Student Story	*"Try cooking some simple snacks (like cheesy nachos) for your housemates while everyone's about just before dinner - it's a great 'pick-you-up' after 5pm lectures on a Friday evening!"*
	Paul, Sociology with Criminology, University of York

Freshers' Week

University kicks off with Freshers' Week. Depending on where you study and what you get involved in this could mean participating in some long held traditions and initiations or just a very social week or two! Freshers' week is a full on multisensory introduction to the extremes of student culture. There is no entering the water slowly, it requires taking a deep breath and jumping in at the deep end! However, before you start to panic, if you follow the advice that has been shared by some experienced swimmers in this book we think you'll soon be enjoying the very best of what university has to offer.

See also Boundaries

Friendships

University is a unique life stage in which you encounter more people in a close social setting than you will do at any other time. Enjoy making friends with a wide variety of people and you will probably learn a lot more about the world in a short space of time. Don't be surprised if your friendship groups evolve and change as you get to know people more. You may find you later connect with certain people who you weren't initially drawn to or vice versa.

It is worth stating that friendship isn't a right, it's a gift. We receive friendship when people offer friendship to us and we give our friendship to others. We can't demand or control friendships but we can cultivate and nurture them through being kind, considerate and consistent. The best friendship that you can offer is when you are being yourself. It is this authentic approach that builds trust and lays the foundation for long term and fulfilling friendships.

Gap Years
to Gym

Gap Years

Some people choose to have a gap year before university and others do one later in life. If you have done a gap year already you'll have some stories to tell and will have already experienced what life looks like away from home. Be gracious to those who are only just discovering what it looks like to fend for themselves, it's likely you will have done a lot of maturing over your gap year and now it's their chance to discover their independence.

God

God wants to be intrinsically woven into your life throughout your years at university. He wants to walk with you, laugh with you, cry with you and do life with you. If you let him, the next three or more years will be a portion of your life in which you see amazing things happen for God's kingdom. The more you let God into your life, the more he can work in you and through you, and the more fulfilling uni life will be.

Gossip

Gossip can be addictive, interesting, funny, insightful and exciting, but in all the wrong ways. People spend hours on gossip websites every day. Why? I believe it's because we have this hunger for little snippets of information about others that make us feel better about our own lives. Gossiping is destructive and a good example of how the tongue can be used to destroy rather than build up.

I challenge you to decide that you are not going to take part in destructive conversations. Create strategies to put in place if you find yourself amidst gossip. Maybe you actively defend the person or quickly change the subject. James 3:1-12 warns about how the tongue is a powerful tool, which can be used to build up or destroy. Where gossip is taking place, try saying something positive about the person who is being targeted. Make sure you use your words to build a person up where you can and build a reputation as someone who doesn't indulge in gossip.

Graduation

Something we are all aiming for I hope! Work hard with your eyes fixed on this goal and be sure to have a lot of fun on the way. You'll be donning that gown and funny hat in no time and wondering where all the time went!

Student Story

"I just graduated this year and I can't believe how fast it went. Just make the most of every opportunity you have. I'd definitely do it all over again!"

Jessica, Physiotherapy, University of Liverpool

Gym

Body image - we all have one. The question is, are we conforming to how the world wants us to look? Or, are there other motivations for going to the gym? Either way, let's talk fitness for a moment. Did you know that looking after our bodies is a way of glorifying God? After all, if our bodies are temples of the Holy

Spirit, surely we should look after them? If walking up a flight of stairs sets your heart racing, then maybe a bit of exercise would be a good idea. We are meant to be doing at least two-and-a-half hours of exercise per week, be that walking at a fast pace to a few lectures or joining a sports club.

When it comes to gyms, have a think before you rush into joining one. Realistically, how often will you go? Have you been a member of a gym before? If so, did you go enough times to justify payment? I signed up to a gym for a year with the full intention of going at least three times a week. And I did... for about a week! When reviewing my gym membership at the end of the year, I was told that on average, I had been twice a month. Oops. If I do the maths that's nearly £15 per visit! Considering that all I did was a few minutes on the treadmill before rushing towards the sauna for what I was convinced was a well-earned rest, it's really quite embarrassing.

You don't have to sign up to a three year gym membership to stay fit at university! Why don't you don your trainers and go for a run or make the most of free sports groups like ParkRun available locally. Whatever you do, be creative and think of ways you can keep your whole body in good shape and have fun too.

Hall Food to Housemates

Hall Food

If you are in a catered hall you will soon learn the wonders of hall food. My experience was good, I enjoyed it and found there to be a wide variety of things to choose from. Breakfast gave the option of a 'full English' for those who were up early enough, lunch offered a variety of hot and cold food, and dinner was a choice between three or four main meals. It is definitely not Michelin star, but it's better than school dinners!

Sometimes, however, the meals are at certain times and you might end up spending more on extra food so that you can get to everything you want to do. If you've already signed up to catered halls, plan your time and money wisely in case you miss meals. If not, work out whether cooking in a non-catered hall would be a better option for your lifestyle and budget.

Halls of Residence

Catered, self-catered, off campus, on campus. Chances are whatever hall you are in, it will become a social hub from which friendships are formed and you will learn a whole lot more about people and yourself. There is no escaping this greenhouse environment, both yours and other people's lives are on display. Through mood swings and loud music, conflicts and coffees, faith, fun and friendship can be shared and deepened. You may find yourself in a hall, a corridor or a flat with a random mix of people who you will have to live life with for a year! This may be an exciting or excruciating prospect. Either way, I challenge you to make the most of your living arrangements. You will probably have opportunities to make friends from all over the world, to get to know people really well, and also an opportunity to influence.

Start praying about your hall, where you will live, and the people you will live among. Ask God to give you an insight into how you can make a difference and be a positive witness for him. It is quite probable that most, if not all, will have no idea how much God loves them. Get to work living, loving and serving – what an opportunity! Consider starting a small group in your hall or running an Alpha course.

See also Doorstop

Student Story

"I looked around at the people I was with in halls and instantly compared them to my friends back home, finding that none of them 'matched up'. Panic set in - how was I supposed to live with these people for a year, maybe more? They were nothing like me. A few weeks in some friendships will begin to blossom and you will certainly find people you click with - if not in your flat then in the flats around you. My advice would be to stick it out, keep praying, and wait for God to reveal some amazing friends you just didn't see there before."

Beth, History and Politics, University of Sheffield

Holidays

Holidays – those lovely breaks between semesters and terms. Unlike the six week summer holidays that school offered, you will have to get used to a three month long summer extravaganza. What's more you get a further month off for Easter and Christmas. Wow! What to do with all that time! In total you have approximately five months away from uni, which leaves only seven months for university.

For me it was a mixture of time spent earning money, going on mission trips, and holidaying during my three mammoth summers. Choose to spend your time outside of university semesters wisely. Christmas and Easter often mean there is coursework, essays and revision to do. However, you will still have more time than at any other point in your life, so it is worth thinking and planning ahead to make the most of it.

See also Easter Holiday

Homesickness

Feelings of homesickness are really common during the first few weeks and occasionally months at university. In most cases the feelings pass fairly quickly, so it is important that you don't make hasty decisions to leave because of your feelings.

Phone home when you need to, but also look locally for relationships that will help you. Fusion work with dozens of local churches in every university location that are wanting to support you during those first few weeks and sometimes difficult days at university. To make the transition to university a lot easier make contact with some churches and student workers now using the Student Linkup App.

Student Story

"In my first term, I really missed home. I wanted to leave at first, but my parents encouraged me to stick it out. They eventually caved in and I went back for a few days. I felt a bit stupid, because I realised that nothing had changed and it was actually a bit boring. The grass is always greener, hey! I felt much more settled within a few weeks. "

Ryan, Education Studies, Leeds Metropolitan University

House Parties

I will never forget the first house party we had. In my second year at university some friends and I moved out of halls and into a house. We decided it was a perfect opportunity for a 'housewarming' party. It was great fun of course, but once everything had died down at about 5am (after I had kicked some lads out of the kitchen who were discovering that fried cheese was apparently quite delectable), there were some interesting revelations. One of the girls had previously made a rather large, pink cake, which I discovered had now taken residence across the wall. Don't even ask me how it got into the washing machine. After some hard work cleaning up, I stopped for a bite of lunch only to find we had a severe shortage of forks, but soon discovered them thrown out of the window and contorted into all sorts of 'bent' shapes. Our microwave was 'held at ransom' and there was some conspicuous yellow water in the kettle (apparently this is a tradition).

House parties are brilliant fun, but need to be thought about. If you are going to have a large number of people, consider making it a pre-club party. This will ensure that your house is not occupied until ridiculous hours, and will significantly reduce mess! Also, think about any doors which may need to be locked, and things which may need to be hidden – valuables, sharp objects. Remember also that you have paid a deposit on your house and your landlord will be expecting you to leave it as you found it. Oh, and hide your kettle!

Housemates

In your first year at university you don't get to choose your housemates, but for the rest of university you do, so choose wisely. Choosing your housemates in your second and third years is a great chance to live out the gospel and share your life and faith with friends who don't yet know Jesus. Think through who you want to live with – living with Christians may seem like an easier option, but is it what God is calling you to in this season? If you're convinced it is, how will you use your house to bless your other mates and avoid becoming an insular Christian bubble?

Also, you can't control your housemates' behaviour, but you can decide what kind of a housemate you will be. Make a choice to be generous, kind, a listening ear and an encourager from the outset. What words would you use to describe the kind of housemate you'd like to be? If you're stuck for ideas, think about what kind of housemate you'd like and work with that!

Instagram to Insurance

Instagram

Social media has changed the world. It records, if you let it, every moment, every thought and every action and with all the pictures to prove it. It keeps us connected, in the loop and up to speed.

However, be aware! It may also change your future. The photos you hoped would be restricted to the relatively carefree culture of university are now being viewed by potential employers. Those comments and opinions that seemed like a good idea at the time have long since been forgotten, but not deleted. Social media users need both wisdom and self-control.

Here are our top 3 social media tips:

1. Think before you post.

2. Don't say online the things that need to be said face to face.

3. Do limit the amount of time you spend on social media.

Intramural Sport

Some universities have an intramural league, which enables halls to compete against each other in a variety of sports. This can be anything from football to basketball or chess to darts. This gives opportunity for people to get involved in fun and competitive sports who may not be good enough to play for university sports teams. It is a great way to get to know more people in your hall and keep fit, so pack some sports clothes and join in!

Initiations

You may or may not have heard of club initiations. They are often creatively dreamed up by team execs to initiate new club members into sports teams or onto committees. They can range widely from singing a silly song, to rather boisterous activities involving vast amounts of alcohol and nakedness!

I have spoken to many students who have wished to get involved in a team or committee but have absolutely dreaded the initiations. They haven't wanted to get drunk or compromise their values and they are absolutely right to stick to their convictions. We have heard some creative solutions to initiations which we'd love to share with you. For example, people not being pressured to drink, people refusing to drink and not being hassled about it, people finding that there are other Christians on the team through not drinking. A friend of mine who was up for a laugh said he'd drink milk instead of beer – it was still very messy! You see, it isn't about not joining the team out of fear of the initiation or about avoiding the initiation and missing out on some crazy socialising. It's about being salt and light. Go, but put your foot down when you are being asked to do something you feel uncomfortable about, and be open about explaining why! Pray about it and use it as an opportunity to witness to your fellow team mates. As well, ask another Christian friend to pray for you and be accountable to them.

See also Alcohol

Insurance

It is worth considering insuring your bike, laptop, phone and gadgets when you leave home. Some insurance is included in student deals with banks or houses and some insurance companies might offer a competitive student rate. Do research your options and discuss it with your parents, you might already be covered!

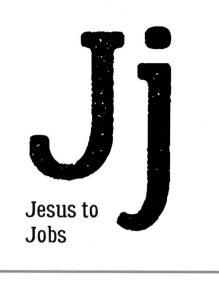

Jj

Jesus to Jobs

Jesus

We get to read about the life of Jesus in the Bible. He showed us how to live, love people, love parties and still be friends with God. We are called to follow Jesus. Live in a way that reflects how he would live, speak how he would speak, and love like he would love. If Jesus were studying at your university, which clubs and societies would he join? Where would he hang out? Who would be his friends? Where would he confront the culture? How would he use social media? What would his devotional life look like? Who would he eat and drink with??

What I've discovered is that whilst most students aren't interested in Christianity as a religion, they are intrigued by those who authentically follow Jesus and call him their friend. How will you share Jesus with people at university?

Student Story

"You'd be surprised how many people are quite interested in Jesus. Even at a purely intellectual level he's fascinating. I've had so many great conversations with people who love talking about Jesus and what he was like, but who would probably get completely put off by the idea of a chat about Christianity, just because of the baggage that goes along with that label."

Paul, History, University of Cambridge

Jobs

Remembering why you applied for university in the first place and the reason you are taking on significant student debt keeps you focussed. Hopefully, university will help open the door to a job where you can make a meaningful contribution. However, the biggest investment of this time and money is not in knowledge but in you. How you change and grow as a person during the university years can either make you someone everyone wants to employ or not! Use the opportunities you have to study hard and hone your skills as well as to grow in self awareness and emotional intelligence. These are traits that mean even if you aren't sure exactly what you want to do, your character and work ethic will be welcome in many places.

Kettle to Kitchens

Kettle

You may think 'what is 'kettle' doing in here?' But I want to give you a nice practical tip – take a kettle for your room! Be a tea and coffee maker. Everyone loves a tea break, it takes anything between five and fifteen minutes to drink and you can get to know the people who live around you much better. A kettle helps you to practice both servant heartedness and listening skills! If you have a kettle in your kitchen, do a tea and coffee round for people in your corridor or house.

Kitchens

Student kitchens are notorious for being one of the most unhygienic rooms in a house or hall, often closely followed by the bathroom. Rather than get annoyed, practice some secret acts of service and every now and again, roll up your sleeves and power through those dirty piles of washing up. It will bless your friends, keep you own attitude healthy and make your place more enjoyable to hang out in! In halls, you may have a cleaner but they won't do everything – try and keep things fairly tidy. Often the best thing to do is to clean up after yourself, and perhaps even others, as you go.

Landlords to Love

Landlords

Up until now, the only landlord you have possibly known is your parents and they have probably protected you from the responsibility of running a house. Student landlords are a mixed bag and can range from the unscrupulous to the very helpful. Before signing a contract it is recommended that you find out the experience of previous tenants. You should also read the contract carefully and, if unsure, show it to your parents. Often Student Unions or universities will have contracts available that give you an indication for what you should look for and that have a bias towards the tenant. Sometimes the smaller independent landlords give a much better service and will have lower rentals than landlords letting through estate or letting agents. Student housing doesn't tend to be in short supply, so don't rush to find a house in your first term before Christmas, make sure you look around and ask lots of questions.

Lectures

It's what you're there for right? The variety in timetables is amazing, compare yours with someone else's and you will see that some people have two lectures a week, and some have twenty-five. However, those with fewer lectures will find a higher importance placed on 'extra reading' and will require more self-motivation. University lectures and seminars should be a priority, you have paid lots of money for them and on a course with fewer lectures that could equate to as much as £250 per lecture!

Colossians 3:23 says, 'Work willingly at whatever you do, as though you were working for the Lord rather than for people.' We are told to put our all into what we do, whether that is a piece of coursework or sticking to our timetable. Our coursework, when done with an attitude that wants to glorify God, is worship! Give yourself time to study, time to work, time to revise, and time to enjoy yourself in the full knowledge that all you do is for God.

Library

Google will get you so far, but do go and check out the library within the first month! Familiarise yourself with the section of books, journals and resources for your specific course and modules. Find out how the online system works and ask for help if you need it. There are often loads of extra services offered by the library too – workshops, tutorials, extra study help and careers advice. Get into the habit of using the library and going there for a few hours once or twice a week. It is good to have a few different working environments and a place you may even call home during certain seasons of your university life.

Locks

Bike locks, door locks, house locks. Sadly students can be a target for crime so always make sure you lock windows and doors. It sounds obvious but if you're all going on a night out make sure the last person to leave knows to lock up! Or if you're having BBQs in the summer and you need to stock up on ketchup, remember to lock up – even if you're just nipping next door!

Often in halls of residence, the doors are fire doors and will shut and lock automatically. If you're leaving your room to chat to a friend, remember your keys or your warden might get fed up after the tenth time!

Lastly, if you've got a bike at university, invest in a good lock for it. Often during the first few weeks there is opportunity to have it registered and marked by the police.

Loneliness

University is often described as the place you'll meet your best friends for life – and for lots of people that's true, but in the first few weeks when everything's turned upside down it is easy to feel lonely in a crowd of people. If this is what you experience, then know that this is really normal and you're not on your own. There are a number of people who really need your friendship, so be brave and make the first move in being a friend to others. Take an interest in their life and ask lots of questions, very soon that interest will be reciprocated and you will find yourself surrounded by new friends.

Clubs and Societies are a great way to meet people with similar interests to you. Don't be scared of extending invitations – asking for a coffee or inviting someone round to watch a movie. There are lots more people struggling with loneliness than is obvious by appearances.

See also Homesickness

Love

God's primary and most glorious attribute is that of love. This love is not a concept or a romantic ideal but an eternal, enduring, sacrificial love that causes hardened hearts to melt and cynics to dance. If an advertising agency were charged with branding this love they would struggle. A specific group cannot be targeted on the basis of their income, background, apparent worth or contribution to society. God's love doesn't carry a price tag to receive it or an education to understand it. It mysteriously clings to his followers, inseparable through life's highest points and darkest days.

In order to love our universities we must learn from the life of Christ how to speak loving words, show loving actions and perform loving wonders. The ministry of Jesus both proclaimed and demonstrated the good news of the kingdom. Christ was and still is the message he embodied. He used words, works and wonders to convince the world of this fact.

Our universities and the students they hold need loving like never before. Will you be part of a generation God is raising up and share God's love with the university?

Student Story

"In our church, we wanted to be very deliberate about sharing God's love with students. It is a really simple message to students: Jesus loves you; we want to show you some of that love and, if you're interested, let's get to know each other and you can find out more. You can do anything from fixing people's bikes, handing out free water to sticking a sofa on campus to be available to talk about anything. I love it when sharing my faith feels like it comes naturally and it's fun!"

Kelly, English, Loughborough University

Marks to Mobile Phones

Marks

Your first few terms at university are ones the lecturers use to get students up to speed and sometimes they do use shock tactics. In the first piece of work that was handed back to my class only a handful of students managed more than 10% – definitely shocking! I did social psychology, and after doing an A level in psychology, the lecture content was not alien to me. However, some of my course friends had done A-levels that had very little in common with social psychology. Lecturers are fully aware that students will take a bit of time to learn what is expected of them in regards to coursework and assignments.

Give yourself a bit of grace to begin with and work hard to understand the marking system tutors use. So when you get back a mark you were not expecting, or a grade that has confused you, think about the following:

- Did you do your best at this piece of work?

- Read the comments made by the marker and take them into account. Often tutors spend a lot of time giving feedback which never gets read. Your tutor knows the subject inside out, and so their feedback should be valuable and reliable.

If your mark has confused you and you feel as if you deserved better, do not be afraid to organise a quick meeting with your tutor to go over the mark. You should go away understanding the mark, or in some cases have a revised mark.

Mates

The people who you hang around with will be paramount to your growth and your impact as a Christian. Make sure you are spending quality time with Christians who are able to challenge you and encourage your growth, and that can build you up so you have the strength of values to be a positive influence on unchurched mates.

Unfortunately, a minority of Christians end up with only Christian friends at uni. They only join clubs with the word Christian in the title and spend most days of their week in one form of Christian meeting or another. It feels holy, but it isn't. Be a mate to those who don't yet know Jesus and prioritise time with them – it will keep you and your Christian life interesting and effective.

A practical way to outwork this is when you are choosing mates to live with. When it comes to renting a student house, don't sign up for a house with solely Christian occupants by default. Be intentional and missional in your choices. There is something very powerful about living with a mixture of non-Christians and Christians. Your life will be on show, and your actions will speak loudly.

See also Bubble and Housemates

Student Story

"Don't make my mistake and end up in Christian bubble world. I was really passionate about being a missionary to my mates but I ended up going about it completely the wrong way. People saw my passion, and they had good intentions, but I wasn't very good at saying "no" and before I knew it, I was going to every Christian group and on every Christian committee you could think of. It took me ages to get out of those commitments and actually start spending some quality time with my friends who didn't know Jesus yet. My advice is to get stuck into a local church but stay sharp about the balance of time you're spending around Christians. Saying yes to one thing always means you're saying no to something else."

Lisa, *Modern Language Studies, University of Nottingham*

Mission Styles

Evangelism could be seen as helping people learn about Jesus and how to relate to him. When we are sharing our faith, or someone is wanting to find out more about Jesus, it's very similar to a learning process - and we all learn in different ways. Mission Styles is an online test and resource to help each of us discover how we most naturally share Jesus. It is also a tool to help us learn how to share our faith with other people who might be wired differently to us. As part of your preparation for university why not take the test at missionstyles.org

Mobile Phones

Mobile phones are almost a part of us now and we are rarely more than two feet away from the one we own. They are fantastic for keeping in contact with friends and texting Mum and Dad to let them know how life at uni is going.

However, just like banks, mobile phone companies will be coming at you with all sorts of attractive offers. When finances are tight, do you really need an upgrade?

Here are some money saving tips for you and your mobile:

- When looking at contracts, think about usage! Are you a texter or a caller? Or are you both? Some contracts offer unlimited text messages, where as some give you an 'allowance' which is a flexible option in which you aren't tied in to using a certain amount of texts or calls.

- Use WiFi when possible. Your university and halls of residence will have good WiFi coverage, and it's included in many student house contracts. Don't pay out for big data packages and then find you don't need them.

- Keep a track on your data usage. You can often set up alerts with your contract provider to remind you when you are approaching your usage limit. This will ensure you don't end up with a nasty surprise at the end of the month.

- Be aware of extra bundles and charges. For example, if you are abroad, you pay to both make and receive calls. Plus, some companies cheekily attach 'free bundles' without making it clear that they're only free for a month or two, but then continue on at a cost! When you sign a contract, read it and ask the salesperson to explain everything to you.

See also Budgets

Nicknames to Notes

Nicknames

You have probably had a few nicknames growing up that may or may not suit you now. However, you're just about to meet a whole load of people who don't know you or your history and if you form some good friendships, expect a new nickname. It is customary in many sports teams for nicknames to be assigned and then embroidered onto the back of a shirt. Most are fun and a sign that you have integrated well into uni life and found some good mates! If you're not happy with a nickname because it's rude or hurtful, make sure you don't let it stick and be confident enough to confront the issue. It's likely it'll be something fun and maybe with a good story attached to it!

Notes

Fusion doesn't advocate that you miss a lecture, but just occasionally it happens. If you can't make a lecture, make sure you get the notes. By the time exams come around you'll be very glad of a full set of notes! It's a good idea to review every lecture so that you remember the content. For all you device geeks there are a bunch of apps out there to help you file and organise.

Student Story

"I'm a bit of a geek and love making really good notes in lectures; coloured pens, illustrations, the lot. They were so good; everyone wanted a copy, so I 'sold' them to my mates in exchange for drinks, (a mixture of alcoholic and non-alcoholic of course)."

Kate, Chemical Engineering, Imperial College London

Offers to Opportunities

Offers

If you've applied to uni, it isn't going to be long before you start receiving some offers. Many of these will be 'conditional', which means that you have to achieve certain grades to be accepted on the course. Don't panic if you miss out on the grades, the world isn't going to end. Trust that God has a plan for your life and that our first choices aren't always the best or only option for us anyway!

Online Food Shopping

Shopping for food online could save you time and money. Club together in your flat and buy your food each week in one online shop (without plastic bags of course!). The delivery cost will be cheaper than all getting buses or taxis with your heavy food bags, you're less likely to impulse buy (ooh, a pineapple!) and you can easily share big bags of pasta, bread, milk etc. if you wanted to.

Opportunities

The Message version of Colossians 4:2-6 (with added emphasis), says: "Pray diligently. Stay alert, with your eyes wide open in gratitude. Don't forget to pray for us, that God will open doors for telling the mystery of Christ, even while I'm a student on campus. Pray that every time I open my mouth I'll be able to make Christ plain as day to them. Use your heads as you live and work among outsiders. Don't miss a trick. Make the most of every opportunity. Be gracious in your speech. The goal is to bring out the best in others in a conversation, not put them down, and not cut them out."

Making the most of every opportunity isn't about us getting worked up to evangelise, it's about us living mission-shaped lives with Christ at the centre. Mission isn't an event or activity, it is a lifestyle and one that takes every opportunity to reveal to people how much God loves them.

The university years are abundant in opportunities for witness. God wants to use you in ways you never imagined but that will make you feel fully alive. With seven months of uni and five months of holiday, it is quite probable that you will have more opportunities presented to you than at any other time of your life.

Part-Time Work to Pub Crawl

Part-Time Work

For some, your loan is a nice handy bit of pocket money, but for most it has to stretch a long way! If you need your loan to pay for accommodation and fees, you may find that you need a part-time job to make up the deficit. According to the NUS, 70% of students work part-time whilst studying. If you need a job, take these things into consideration:

- How much do you need to / would you like to earn?

- How much time do you have available to work? Consider that you will need to use some of your free time to do coursework and revision.

- Will you be able to commit to a job over semester holidays?

- Will your employer mind you going home over the holidays?

- How many hours would you want to work? Ensure that your employer is aware of this.

Don't forget that your university will have a careers advice centre, and people available to help you with sorting out your finances and work. There are many jobs for students available on campus and in shops.

Pot Noodle

I understand that to some slightly lazy or busy students there is something rather attractive about the Pot Noodle. Its packaging is interesting and it's a meal in a cup! Genius. All you need is a kettle (you will rarely be out of sight of one) and enough strength to peel back the foil. The only problem is the three minutes waiting time in which the dried peas and noodles need to soften enough to eat, unless you like them al dente that is.

However, unfortunately, a pot noodle is not the healthiest thing you can live off. It contains little of the nutrients you need (no, the five peas floating on the top do not count as your five a day) and will be doing your insides no good. Do your loved ones a favour and spend a little time before you go to uni learning a few simple recipes and cooking skills. You probably won't become 'master chef' but at least you won't need to eat out of a pot.

Pre-Drinks

Pre-drinks is often where a night out begins. It's cheaper than buying drinks in a bar/pub/club but it does mean that some students are arriving in town at the start of the night already drunk. Pre-drinks doesn't have to be booze-filled, the smaller group setting and (slightly) quieter music means it can be a great time to actually get to know people before heading into town.

There is already a reaction to a culture that prioritises drunkenness and leaves students heading into town already vulnerable and out of control. A third (33%) of students don't drink alcohol at all. Not drinking is a great option.

See also Alcohol and Drinking games

Pub Crawl

A staple of the fresher's week celebrations and a common society social, pub crawls do what they say on the tin. A long list of pub visits rounded off, usually, in one of the town's reputable clubs. This can be a very social form of drinking as the group and conversations get mixed up from place to place. But if you do drink it is easy to lose track of how much alcohol you're consuming. Alternating water, soft drinks and alcohol is a good way to not drink excessively. Being sober on these sorts of socials is a great option, and means that you may be needed to help your mates get home safely after a night of disorientating trekking around.

See also Alcohol and Initiations

Quality Time to Quitting

Quality Time

At university you are constantly surrounded by people. I want to stress the importance of spending time alone with God too. This may be easy for some as it is a natural part of your day and you desire quiet periods to stay sane! For others, you may thrive on social contact and find it an effort to be alone for long enough to get your Bible out! Jesus spent regular time alone. Why? Because he liked it? Absolutely! But I believe it was also because he knew the importance of spending time with his Father in Heaven.

Whether it is 'quiet' or 'loud' time, the heart behind it is quality time alone with God. In my quality time, God realigns things for me. I know that if I go a few days without it, I can tell in my behaviour and my thought life. I know that God yearns to spend time with me, yet sometimes I am so easily distracted. Decide on a regular set time each day that you can spend with God. This may be the morning, or it may be the evening, but make it a priority in your day and make sure you're alert. Someone once said, 'today I am very busy, so I must pray more'. They realised the importance that the busier we are, the more we need God in our day! Yet I sometimes use busyness as an excuse not to pray or spend time with God!

Think about journaling. Some people find it a useful way to write down and record prayers and thoughts. Not 'today for dinner I ate…' but deeper, more important things. There is something very powerful about looking back at prayers which have been prayed and answered, and changes in our character which have been made over time.

Quitting

This is probably not what you want to read about before starting uni. However, we all feel like quitting from time to time – so don't be surprised if these feelings happen to you. Talk and pray with a friend or someone at your church. Most often these feelings pass fairly quickly.

See also Homesickness

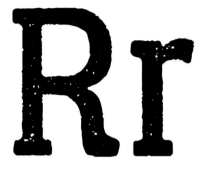

Reading Lists to Rooms

Reading Lists

Reading lists vary depending on the course but you'll break the bank if you try buying all the books all first-hand. Try finding second hand copies online or buying them from students who don't need them anymore, and check if you have access to any online through your uni. If you keep them in fairly good condition, you can sell them onto new freshers next year too! But, if you're going to risk not buying them and count on the library, make sure you have a look early before everyone else has taken them out on loan!

Referencing

Your tutors or library will offer you plenty of advice on referencing so don't panic! It's possibly a completely new technique for you but you'll pick it up soon enough. When you're writing an essay, it's a good idea to keep reference notes or write the bibliography as you go; otherwise you might forget where all the best points came from if you leave it to the end!

Relationships

Many people start university hoping to find a 'relationship' but, in reality, this means so much more than meeting a boyfriend/girlfriend. University is a fantastic opportunity to form a range of great new friendships and relationships; find new mates, meet inspiring mentors both within uni and in the local church. You can also have a positive influence on the people around you. When you think about relationships, in whatever context, ask yourself; 'what can I give?' as much as 'what do I need?'

Religions

People will be coming to your university from all over the country and the world, bringing with them different sets of values and beliefs. Be open, interested and ready to learn about people and what they believe. God wants everyone to discover how much he loves them. Love people and show an interest in their lives, customs and beliefs. Whether you agree or not, listen and take time to ask questions about what people believe in. If you are living with or studying with someone from another faith, take the time to do a bit of research into their beliefs to understand more about what they live for. Developing friendships with those who profess another faith or religion will sharpen your own faith and we must be ready to articulate why and what we believe about Jesus.

Re-set

Whilst it's true that first impressions can be hard to shift, it's also true that it's never too late to start afresh if you find yourself on a road you're not happy with. Lots of students make bad lifestyle choices, often contradicting their faith and beliefs. Sometimes they head off track and aren't sure how to get back. We have a God who puts no restrictions on who and when people can turn back to him – he is always waiting with arms open to help you get back on track and work out what it means to be a follower of Jesus in this new culture. James speaks about confessing your sins to one another. The quickest way to get back on track is to do this with a trusted friend and re-set your heart on Jesus.

Rooms

What's in your room will declare more about you than you realise. It will make statements about the things you value and the people you care about. Consider what impact your room has on other people when you start to personalise it. It'll be bare when you arrive but you can take photos, posters, lights, duvet covers, or plants with you to brighten it up and make it your own. Be mindful of using Blu Tack and leaving marks on the walls – you'll appreciate that room deposit back! It also makes sense to make your room a bit of a sanctuary so when you close the door and you are on your own you enjoy spending time there.

Secret Sin to Student Housing

Secret Sin

One of my friends in my hall had a pretty gross practical joke played on him. Another guy had secretly placed some raw fish into an open Tupperware container far underneath his bed. He was a messy guy, so pretty soon the Tupperware was covered with clothes, books and rubbish. As I am sure you can imagine the smell started to spread. Weeks later (yes weeks – and bear in mind this was in summer time!) he stank. The smell was no longer simply in his bedroom, it had got into his clothes and his skin. He may have been used to the smell, but we weren't.

Unfortunately, it took us a while to work out the root of the disgusting odour, and once we did, he had to air and clean his room a fair few times before the stubborn smell began to dissipate!

Satan adores secret sin because, like the raw fish smell, it can grow to pervade every fibre of our being. It is in the dark places where the mould can grow, and secret sin will fester. We keep sin a secret because we fear people's responses and are ashamed. We might even reason, 'you like me/love me/befriend me, but not if you knew who I really am…' Secret sin entangles us and enslaves us. Like the raw fish, the longer it is kept in the dark, the worse it gets. It may be a negative habit, an unhealthy way of thinking, bad treatment of ourselves…we have all been there.

Throw open the curtains, let the sunshine come in. Accountability and discipleship throws the light into the dark places and puts things back into perspective. Step out of secret sin by confessing it both to God and to someone who cares about you and desires to see you grow. We are called to be children of light (Ephesians 5:8). Know that you are living under grace filled, unconditional love.

Seek accountability and embrace vulnerability. You are not called to get through things on your own, but with the strength and help of God and faithful friends.

See also Accountability

Student Story

"I'd been struggling with some stuff even before I came to uni, but never really talked about it. Somehow, I felt embarrassed talking to people I'd known for ages. When I came to uni and joined a local church, I felt like because people didn't know me in the same way, I could make a new start. I decided to open up to one of my new friends in my church small group. It felt so freeing to be honest and open. We're keeping each other accountable and I feel like I'm getting back on track with being the real me."

Sarah, Economics, University of Warwick

Sex

Why don't Christians have sex before marriage? How does this question make you feel? Does it make you shudder or do you see it as an opportunity to speak confidently about what you value? Below are a few principles to consider as you prepare for university and think about how you may answer this question.

1. You will encounter a lot of people who confuse sex with love and probably don't understand the true meaning of either. Love is self-sacrificing, self-controlled, values the other person and is gentle. If it's 'just sex', it's none of these things.

2. If you're being pressured to have sex, this is neither loving or selfless. Is this relationship one with God at the centre at all? God has given you everything you need to say no to this pressure and to make a stand to live life differently. If you are currently in a sexual relationship, it's not too late. God is able to restore sexual purity and help us set new boundaries. Talk to someone you trust.

3. Deciding to not have sex until you are married will put you in the minority at university. Think about how you will share your views confidently. GK Chesterton said, "right is right even when nobody is doing it and wrong is wrong even when everybody is doing it." Not everything is relative. God knew what he was doing when he gave the gift of sex to be a blessing in marriage.

Sharing

…is caring, as they say. This is true and it's really special if you can share food and time with your friends and housemates. Serving each other is humbling and peace-bringing, and is so helpful for living in harmony with one another. It's hard to be angry with someone who's just cooked you dinner! I found communal dinners to be such an important time to check in with my housemates and make sure I had some good social contact on the busy days. It also kept my food costs down as I only cooked once or twice a week! It's worth discussing, probably earlier than later, which household items (washing up liquid, toilet roll etc.) you're going to share and how you're going to split the cost so one person doesn't end up paying for it all.

Shopping

We live in a culture where we can buy pretty much anything we want to with a few clicks of a mouse. Shopping is easy, and we're surrounded by a message of materialism. We're constantly being told that 'things' will improve our lives and complete us, whether that's a top that we feel is destined to end up in our wardrobe, or it's a new range of gourmet pasta sauces that we think put last week's meals to shame. If we buy into this mentality we'll be constantly searching for the next thing and never satisfied. Once the top has been worn twice it won't feel as new any more and we'll be on the lookout for the next thing that will complete our wardrobes.

Contactless payments and online shopping can be particularly dangerous, as it doesn't even really feel like you're spending any money, and the promise of free returns may lure you in to buying far more than you originally planned to. There's a few things that I think are worth bearing in mind when shopping:

1. Remember that possessions do not complete you or define you.

2. Consider if you're investing into something which will actually be worthwhile. Will it only satisfy your desire for a few days or will you actually make the most of it? Do you really need it?

3. Are you being a good steward of finance? If you're anything like me, I get tempted to spend my money on yet another item of stationery when I already have more than enough, and I know my money could be better spent or invested elsewhere.

See also Budgeting and Clothes

Social Secs

Social Secs are the secretaries of all things social! They are the members of your hall or general exec who plan socials, broadcast themed evenings and demand that you all dress up. Their job is to increase the morale of the team or hall and ensure that you have an action packed fresher and university experience. They determine what hall or group chants are going to be sung – these will often stay in your mind for years to come, often containing a liberal sprinkling of rude words!

For those of you who are socialites and think you would be good at being a social sec, I urge you to go for it! It will be fun, hard work and demanding at times. But also it is great to have someone who loves God in a position that allows them to instil good values and to set the culture. Many Christian students have opted for this responsibility and have changed the way freshers' weeks are conducted so students are built up rather than humiliated. For example, do the big nights out to build comradery, but have a few 'nights in' to deepen community. Often the focus is alcohol and nightlife-based which tends to exclude those who are more introverted, or who prefer nice nights in! Being a social sec means you can lead in building healthy culture and community.

Societies

You will probably find there is so much choice of clubs and societies to join. They are great to join for meeting new friends, keeping active and busy, as well as doing something you enjoy or learning something new! Most universities have a wide, varied and very eclectic list of societies from hiking clubs, cheer leading and music to other things like baking, chocolate society or Harry Potter appreciation!

Societies can be another opportunity to love your university and share Jesus with the friends you make. Don't get so busy that you have no time for study or rest but choose one or two that might help you really invest into friendships and make the most of your free time.

Student Story | *"My advice would be to join a club or society as soon as you get to uni in something you have never done before. It's a great way of making friends and getting stuck into what's going on at uni!"*

Rosie, Education Studies, York St John University

Spirituality

I have heard people say 'I don't believe in God, but I am a spiritual person'. This tells me that although they are not acknowledging God, they are acknowledging that life seems to stretch beyond the physical and the seen.

So how do we view spirituality in the context of the culture you are about to step into? I think we need to recognise that people are sometimes more aware of the 'spiritual' element than they are of God. This will often lead people into dabbling in many different things. I had a friend at university who started going to a spiritualist church because she wanted to contact her dead Auntie. Although I was very wary that this was not 'church' as she called it, it made her aware that there was 'more' to life than just what you see. This led to some amazing conversations with her about God, and how we can experience the love of God in our lives. I also explained that there is a counter-spiritual side which is dangerous and is out to destroy rather than to engage in a passionate and life-transforming way.

People are looking for the reality of God who they can experience and have a relationship with. When any conversation crops up about spirituality, mention how your God is a spiritual God who you can encounter and experience. Tell stories about the times you have experienced God's love. Do not underestimate the power of your story!

Student Story

"I grew up in an area that wasn't very culturally diverse, so I was really looking forward to meeting a wider range of people when I came to uni. Part of me wondered whether people from other faiths might be a bit suspicious or even hostile about the fact that I was a Christian. Actually, I was surprised by how open people are and have found it interesting to talk to other people and learn about their beliefs. Talking about Jesus is a great opener with a lot of people from different faiths. Seems like a lot of people are really interested in him!"

Hannah, Media and Communication, Birmingham City University

Sports Teams

If you don't consider yourself sporty, don't rule out sports teams just yet. As well as the predictable ball sports like football, rugby, cricket, hockey and tennis there are a whole host of other 'sports' to get involved in. These may include some less obvious activities like tiddlywinks through to trampolining and triathlon. Or what about karate, kickboxing or korfball!? Or ever considered gliding, canoeing, fencing or ultimate frisbee?

Some universities are known for their sports teams, and the reputation they hold. It will be easy enough to get involved in a team but more difficult at the higher levels, although standards will vary across universities. So if you fancy trying something new, or if you already have all the skills, get involved! What a brilliant opportunity to get to know people, challenge yourself and have fun. For the more elite sports people among you, there will be a need to work harder at connecting with a church as often training and competing means you aren't available when others are meeting to study, pray and worship.

Student Housing

Cash back, free summer rent, half summer rent, all inclusive, free TV, free WiFi… housing agencies will be using all sorts of tempting tactics to get you to sign their contracts. Here are some pointers for you that should help you when it comes to the housing rush:

- Agencies put pressure on students to sign for a house as early as the Christmas break! You will be told that houses are being signed for quickly and that if you want to get a good house you must do so as soon as possible. This is not exactly correct. There tend to be so many housing agencies in university towns so there are usually houses available even up until the last minute!

- Don't always feel pressured to use student-housing agencies. Look a bit further afield and you may find that general agencies and independent landlords provide cheaper lettings.

- Think about whether you will need to use accommodation over the summer holiday. Some agencies offer half price summer rent, but occasionally you will find that you cannot actually move into the house over the summer.

See also Landlords

Teaching to TV

Teaching

You will have plenty of teaching in lectures so I am talking about bible teaching, where we ask God to speak to us through scripture and be challenged spiritually. Take a few good Christian books with you to university that you can make your way through. Personally, I love subscribing to podcasts and listening to some pretty fantastic talks by inspiring people. This is quick and easy to do and will give you something to listen to on the walk to your lectures! Of course, by settling into a church quickly at university you will receive some bible teaching, however, this is not enough to grow into all that God has for you. You have to take responsibility for feeding yourself. As Christians, the more time we put into our relationship with God, and the more we apply ourselves to learning about him, the more like and closer to Him we will become.

See also Quality Time

Testimony

Your testimony is your story; a story of revelation and a change thanks to God's work in your life. It might be painful to tell. It may contain tale of a major life turn around, or it may begin with 'I grew up in a Christian family…'

When I used to be asked to share my testimony, I would reply with 'I will, but it's a bit depressing'. My testimony contains death, struggles with self-worth and relationships, and often makes listeners cry – as well as myself! So I thought it shouldn't be told! How wrong I was. My testimony is actually a story of hope, a story of how God has been with me in the midst of pain, and a story of how God has travelled through my life with me. It is a powerful story, that speaks to people who are also struggling with difficult times right where they are.

Do not discredit your testimony by saying 'it's boring, it's just average, not much happened'. Remember:

- Your testimony is unique and powerful.

- Whether you became a Christian yesterday, or you have been brought up in a Christian family, your testimony is the story of how knowing God has affected your life, and how he has worked in it.

- Tell your testimony! People love stories, and it's a story that conveys the love, power and grace of God.

- Don't feel the need to 'tie up' your testimony. You are still a work in progress! Talk about how God is currently working in you as you've allowed him into some of the closed off areas of your life and what changes have happened as a result.

In Revelation 12:11 it says that 'they defeated him (Satan) through the blood of the Lamb and the bold word of their testimony'. So go, tell your testimony, because when you do, you are telling the story of God and this has power to defeat the enemy! Not to mention the opportunity to see salvation!

Time

The student world continues to change rapidly and there are so many opportunities that you can give your time to. Tuition fees mean students are understandably prioritising more time for study and many find part-time work.

Out of the many clubs and societies students can join, you realistically only have the time to meaningfully integrate into one Students' Union club. Add to this the huge options for entertainment, relaxation and the impact of technology, how you choose to spend your time as a Christian student is of huge importance. You have 3-4 years to get a degree, pursue some extra-curricular activities, embrace the responsibilities of adulthood, and hopefully make an impact on one of the most clearly defined, largest and least reached people groups – students. In short, time will go quicker than you think, so you want to be intentional about what and who you invest into.

Transport

You might not have thought about this but how are you going to get around at university? It depends on the size of your campus or your location, but are you going to walk or bike? When you get there, maybe look at the bus options especially to save late night library walks on your own. If you have the option to bring a car – consider petrol, parking costs and the environment and whether you could do without. Don't forget you can also get a young person's railcard for discounted train journeys!

Tuition Fees

Up until university your education has probably been free, but degree level education and beyond costs money. Tuition fees are expensive and another reason to take your studies seriously. When you start earning above a certain amount you will have to start paying back your student debt. It is good to be aware of this as the lectures and the course should be high quality and engaging given how much you are paying, and you should make every effort to attend all your designated lectures.

See also Budgeting and Debt

Tutors

They are your friends and will help you, although you might get on better with some more than others. They want you to get the most out of your university education so make the most of them. Also sign up for tutorials with them, they will often tell you when they're available but it's up to you to go and get a meeting! They'll then get to know you better and you'll be able to get help with your work when you need it.

TV Licence

Anyone who downloads or watches BBC programmes, including catch up TV or on iPlayer, must be covered by a TV Licence. You also need to be covered by a TV Licence to watch or record live TV programmes on any channel, including on iPlayer. This applies to any device you use. Check if this is included in your house or halls contract or if you need to sort it yourself before watching any TV and potentially landing yourself a fine.

Union to Unity

Union

If your university is a campus university, it is likely that the Students' Union will be a bit of a social hub. If it isn't, then it is still a very useful amenity. Unions or Student Guilds often contain a nightclub, a bar or two, and offices in which a large part of the administrative side of the SU is carried out. You could probably drop by to the Union to get a coffee, help with careers advice, student services and lots more. Ensure that you know where it is and when it is open, as it will come in handy.

Unity

Unity is something that makes God smile. Christian unity builds up and strengthens the Church, it doesn't tear apart those who may worship differently or hold different theological convictions. Gospel unity celebrates difference and embraces a diversity of churches and Christian student groups.

We don't need to join the same local church or the same Christian group on campus to be unified. We do need to love and speak well of each other and put

Jesus at the centre. Beware of those who claim to be 'right' or who like to divide the Church into theological 'camps', or who speak badly of others in the body of Christ. The Church is one.

"Since God chose you to be the holy people he loves, you must clothe yourselves with tender-hearted mercy, kindness, humility, gentleness, and patience. Make allowance for each other's faults, and forgive anyone who offends you. Remember, the Lord forgave you, so you must forgive others. Above all, clothe yourselves with love, which binds us all together in perfect harmony. And let the peace that comes from Christ rule in your hearts. For as members of one body you are called to live in peace. And always be thankful" (Colossians 3:12-15).

Values to Vows

Values

Our values are what we demonstrate as being important; they consist of ideologies, behaviours and beliefs. Values are the lenses through which we see everything. They will affect what upsets us, what makes us happy, and how we make decisions! We act out of our values. If we value lots of money, we will be greedy and materialistic.

We can say we have one set of beliefs, but live opposite to them because our values affect our behaviour more than our beliefs. To live authentic Christian lives, we need to align our beliefs with our heart values.

In Luke 10:9, we are told that the kingdom of heaven is near! And what's more, Luke 17: 20-21 tells us that the kingdom is amongst us. So therefore, seeing as Jesus is among us, and we are called to be Christ-like believers, we need to start living in a way that reflects the values of his kingdom.

So what does this mean? To reflect and hold kingdom values? Have a look through the beatitudes (Matthew 5:3-11) and the Ten Commandments (Exodus 20:1-17) and identify guidelines and values God desires us to hold. The difficult thing is that there is a constant tension between selfish values and kingdom values. So when we are trying to live out these kingdom values in the student world, we also need to be living out of God's grace for each of us!

Vanity

University culture creates a powerful temptation to 'look good'. It's easy to get the impression that everyone's checking each other out, but in reality, most people are probably too busy worrying what they look like. The Bible tells us not to worry about our bodies or what we wear (Matthew 6). We can be a powerful inspiration to others by living free from keeping up appearances.

Variety

University, like a large box of chocolates, has variety to match and attract all possible tastes. The vast majority of it is to be embraced; the people from different backgrounds and cultures, the lectures and learning, the clubs and societies all combine to make for a diverse and enriching university experience. I encourage you to throw yourself into it, spread your wings and enjoy the variety of university life.

Vows

This may seem a bit extreme, but stay with me. Think self-imposed boundaries, think about the life that you really want to lead but you know that, in the wrong environment, you could let yourself down or just be lazy.

A vow is not so much a goal as a commitment to live in a way that you know is ultimately going to do you good. For example, my friend Caleb vowed not to drink during his first year at university – it was something he knew would help him. Or how about vowing to do something, to encourage someone every day or read the Bible at the start and the end of the day. A vow or two might just help you lead the life you always wanted.

See also Boundaries

Student Story

"I think one of the most important things I did before I came to uni was to really think about why I believe what I believe. I did the Student Linkup Sessions in my youth group and before that, I'd never really thought about why Christians don't have sex before they get married. I probably would have said "because the Bible says so" but I didn't even know where. It was just a rule and, to be honest, I'd never really had the opportunity so it wasn't really a problem. I'm really pleased I did think about it, because now I genuinely see why not having sex before you're married is a better way. If I hadn't got that heart conviction, I think I could have ended up in some difficult situations because attitudes to sex seem to be pretty 'liberal' in halls."

Joseph, Architecture, University of Lincoln

Washing to Works

Washing

Suddenly you notice that the pile of unwashed clothes in the corner of your room is beginning to take over. It's time to do something about it you think… but what?! Your blood pressure rises and you begin to sweat. This has never happened before. Normally you leave it in a pile and lo and behold, it appears 48 hours later, clean and folded.

I am joking, of course, although I know a few guys for whom this has been a reality at the start of university. If you are in halls, it will be likely that you will have communal laundry facilities. Buy some washing powder and have your pound coins ready! Potentially invest in a small clothes horse in case you need to dry your clothes in your room. An iron might come in handy as well, but that might be going too far!

Water

Water saves lives. Lots of Christian students up and down the country are giving out cups of cold water to drunk students after big nights out. Why? Because

God cares and we care and we don't just say that we care, we show that we care. And what starts as an act of kindness has now on many occasions ended with a life being saved.

'And if anyone gives even a cup of cold water to one of these little ones because he is my disciple, I tell you the truth, he will certainly not lose his reward' (Matthew 10:42).

WhatsApp

It's worth downloading WhatsApp for all your group messaging needs. You could have a family group, friends from home group, a group for that presentation you have to do in week 7 and maybe a 'flat 9b group'! It'll save your texts if you need to discuss plenty and a lot of people already have the app. Careful you don't get too distracted by it and watch your internet data allowance too!

See also Mobile Phones

Winter

It could feel like winter comes before freshers' week has barely even finished! Some halls are heated well whilst others are not, especially in an old student house! Have layers to put on and perhaps a hot water bottle for the much colder nights! If most people are in the house, ask when you want to put the heating on so that you're thinking about heating bills together and fairly.

See also Bills

Wonders

Do you believe that miracles, signs and wonders, healings and visions are for today? Do you believe that you are capable of being used by God? John 14:12

says: "I tell you the truth, anyone who has faith in me will do what I have been doing. He will do even more than this, because I am going to the Father."

Be confident that you have been called to be a disciple, called to be a history maker, called to be the facilitator of wonders!

God equips the called. He doesn't call the equipped.
You have been called. You will be equipped.

Throughout the gospel accounts much of the healings Jesus performed happened outside the synagogues. Many times when Jesus was moved with compassion to pray for people, signs of the kingdom followed and the message of the kingdom was proclaimed. Outside of holy huddles, loving wonders must be demonstrated by bold and sensitive students who will pray and prophesy to the lost and the longing.

Student Story

"Me and my friends from church were really passionate about praying for and seeing God heal people. We prayed for loads of people but one evening, in the bar, we prayed for a girl whose knee had been dislocated in a sporting accident. When we prayed it just went 'creeek' and popped back into place! God is amazing!"

Luke, Geography, University of Reading

Words

Jesus says in Luke 6:45 that 'out of the overflow of the heart, the mouth speaks'. His words pointed to a loving and compassionate God and our words should do the same. We must preach the gospel and preach it with loving words, even if at times those words provoke a reaction.

Work Experience

Whether paid or voluntary – even if just for a week or two while you're at home, work experience will help you learn more about yourself and may be a useful addition to your CV. By the time you're in your third year you will be far busier with exams and dissertations. Whether or not your course advises or includes a year in industry, use a holiday or two to get some local work experience.

See also Holidays and Year in Industry

Works

The story Jesus tells of the Good Samaritan is perhaps his clearest illustration of what it means to love our neighbour. To divorce loving words from loving actions is to diminish the gospel message and ignore the second greatest commandment that humanity has been given. This parable is told in response to a question concerning eternal life and is the antidote to and a warning against the narrow religiosity exhibited by the Pharisees.

How might you do something practical to show God's love to your mates and university?

See also Mission

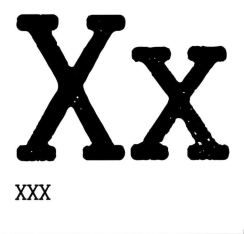

Xx

XXX

XXX – Pornography

Why is porn such a problem? If God has made humanity in his image to reflect his glory, when we treat another human being as an object, or for our own sexual gratification, we diminish and tarnish that image. It affects us too by further alienating us from the opposite sex or the same sex. It inhibits our relationships and reduces our ability to interact with other people.

Porn doesn't even need to be a literal image on a computer; it could be a mental image we dwell on. We are not created for the alienating effects that porn has on us. The fact is you are made for something more and fantasising about another person doesn't fit with who you are. It's what the Bible calls sin and sin always alienates.

It is a massive issue in our culture, including within the church. If you know that you struggle with or are addicted to viewing pornography, make yourself accountable to someone. Give them the right to ask you difficult questions, and ask God for a fresh revelation for how he values people. For help we recommend visiting thenakedtruthproject.com

See also Accountability, Boundaries and Secret Sin

Year in
Industry
to YOLO

Year in Industry

Sandwich course, year out, placement year, year in industry… some courses have them as compulsory, whereas other courses offer optional years out. All I can suggest is that if a year out option is available, take it! If you are hoping to have a career in the discipline of your degree then for employers, it is very attractive for a candidate to have experience in the field of choice. It makes you more employable and adds a practical dimension to the course you study.

If a placement year is something you want to invest in, start applying early. Do your research into which companies do good undergraduate yearly recruitments, and consult your course tutors to get their opinions. Write a good, honest CV that includes every relevant thing you have done, and send it off with an individual cover letter applicable to each company. Look out for companies that may sponsor students on certain courses and provide a placement year as part of that.

"During my year in industry, it was so encouraging when I received emails, calls or messages from my friends in the church I joined in my first year. It made me feel connected and valued. I also managed to find a church near to where I was working thanks to Student Linkup. It was a funny time, because I was working but kind of still a student, so I wanted to find a church that was still passionate about students."

Georgie, Biology, University of Southampton

YOLO

YOLO (you only live once) as a term may be outdated, but the concept and mentality is still rife in our culture. In some ways it can be used to embrace the moment, step out of your comfort zone and have fun. In other ways, this mentality can be very selfish and reckless. If we do not consider the heart behind our actions, or the consequences, we become irresponsible and disconnected. Jesus gives us life to the full, in which many things are to be embraced and enjoyed; he also teaches that with him, we not only live once, but for eternity. This might change the way we act because we are more attentive to who we are becoming for eternity, hopefully more like Jesus, which means owning our decisions and actions.

zzz

zzz – Sleep

Your doctor would prescribe 7-9 hours a night! This gives your body time to recuperate and your mind time to shuffle all your thoughts and memories into the right place (think of a big filing cabinet). During sleep, your neurons can shut down and begin to repair any damage done during the day. If you are awake and alert during the day, then this shows you are getting enough sleep. If you are finding it difficult to get to sleep each night, try the following:

- Cut out caffeine in the late afternoon and evening. Caffeine stays in your system for a good few hours.

- Try to not work in your bedroom. This helps you associate your bedroom with sleeping.

- Avoid alcohol before you sleep. Yes, you do get to sleep faster, but it will prevent you from entering a deep sleep meaning that you wake up unrefreshed.

- Exercise daily.

- Go to bed at the same time every night. Establish a good rhythm of waking and sleeping.

- Wind down – try writing a journal to get your thoughts out on paper, or relaxing by reading a book.

- Avoid looking at screens before you sleep. Even with night settings the light from screens makes it harder to get to sleep. If possible, charge your phone in a different room so it's not tempting to check it as you settle in for the night.

About Fusion

Fusion helps students find hope in Jesus and home in the local church.

Fusion are committed to championing a worldwide movement of student mission. We believe in the power and potency of students as a force for revival and transformation in the world and recognise that university is a key formational, decision making time for them. We are convinced that it is the local church who are best placed to nurture, disciple and support students into mission across campuses, cities and beyond. Fusion therefore seek to equip students for a life of mission and discipleship by guiding them into local churches who are then trained and resourced to effectively care for and release students into the calling God has placed on their lives.

How does Fusion work?

Fusion is fuelling the fires of student movement by:

Equipping Students:

Preparing and inspiring students for a life of mission and discipleship at university.

Serving Churches:

Connecting students into the heart of local church and encouraging churches to be at the heart of student mission.

Developing Student Workers:

Training, resourcing and strengthening all those in church-based student ministry.

Student Linkup

Each year thousands of Christian school leavers go onto a whole new life stage at universities across the UK and the world. Student Linkup prepares, equips and encourages students in their university experience and most importantly, connects them to local church communities in their university location.

Download the Student Linkup App from the App store or Playstore today!

Find out more at fusionmovement.org/app

Resources

Other resources available from fusionmovement.org/resources include:

The Student Linkup Box	360° Preparation for Uni
Discipleship Deck	A pack of cards with 52 challenging discipleship questions
DMC Deck	A pack of cards to start 52 deep and meaningful conversations
Small Groups, Big Mission	A workbook for small group leaders
Student Linkup App - fusionmovement.org/app	Find and connect to a new church at university

Contact us

For more information on our resources and the work of Fusion, contact us at:
Fusion UK, Unit 7, 30 Meadow Lane, Loughborough, LE11 1JY
hello@fusionmovement.org | www.fusionmovement.org | 01509 268 505

Notes & Doodles